This Book Belongs to:

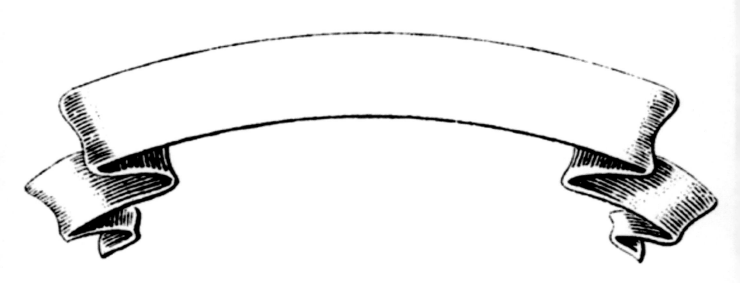

This book is dedicated to my incomparable wife Paloma, my beautiful daughter Kaihlani, and all the fathers that are present & engaged in the lives of their children.

I'll Be Here

Illustrated By: Theophilus Elechi

I'll be here when you're 9.

I'll be here when you're 90.

I'll be here every morning,
With your mommy beside me.

I'll be here when you run.

I'll be here when you fall.

If you need me i'm here,
You just have to call.

At every game you will hear me,
I'll be screaming from the stands.

On the court or off the court,
I'm your biggest fan.

We'll take tons of selfies 1,2,3...
CHEESE!

We'll enjoy mother nature and climb some big trees.

I'll be here to keep you safe,
I'll be here to show you love.

I'll sing songs and dance
while you splash in the tub.

We'll cook a big dinner and talk about our day.

Before going to bed we'll kneel down and pray.

I'll be here when you're 9,
I'll be here when you're 90.

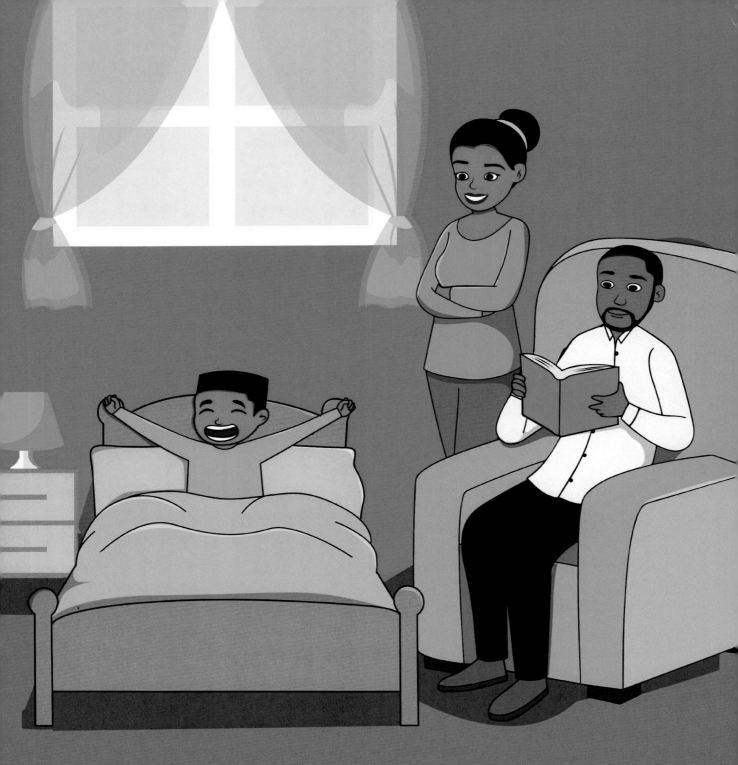

I'll be here every morning,
With your mommy beside me.

No need to have doubts,
no need to have fear.

Because no matter what happens,
I'll be here.

The End

Anthony "Greatness" Cotton is an author, motivational speaker, dancer, and devoted family man. Whether through a speech, book, or dance video, his primary goal is to inspire every person he encounters to BE GREAT. He has worked with children from around the globe, danced on professional television sets, and has been featured in commercials. Anthony is a man of faith, dedicated to his his church, and is on a mission to inspire change and growth in as many lives as possible.

Contact

Email: anthony4cotton@gmail.com

Instagram: @greatnesscotton

Facebook: Anthony Greatness Cotton

Made in the USA
Lexington, KY
26 January 2019